Death

and

Fulness

of

Life

Excerpts from writings and lectures
by
Philip G. Roets STL, SSL
Biblical scholar and teacher, author, educator, counselor,
father, husband, priest, friend and neighbor.

"As I look out on the world of winter,
I see a time of fulfillment
and a time of promise;
a time of challenge
and a time of security;
a time to be treasured
and a time to be used."

from Author's Journal. 12/19/82.

"What legacy do I leave? I started out years ago to let my legacy to be written in the people I serve. I have done this all through the years. Most of the people may not even remember my name but the influence I had on their lives is still going on. That is the legacy I want to leave and am leaving. ." *from Author's Journal. 1/16/91.*

Cover Photography © 1997
by Morris Press

ISBN: 0-911943-82-X
Death and Fulness of Life

Leadership Publishers Inc.
PO Box 8358
Des Moines, Iowa 50301- 8358

Printed in the United States by Morris Publishing
3212 East Highway 30
Kearney, NE 68847
1-800-650-7888

Death and Fulness of Life
by Philip G. Roets STL, SSL
Second Edition

Table of Contents

Purpose of this Book

This book contains thoughts Phil taught and wrote during his lifetime: Biblical commentaries, classes on Old and New Testament, monographs on Biblical themes, and in his daily Journals/Notes to his wife, Lois. Because they give comfort to Lois, they may also give comfort to you.

We (Philip & Lois) share these notes with you. Please share these thoughts with others and add your own insights.

Pre-Notes:

Philip G. Roets already lives in many of us. Phil's insights, wisdom, and perspectives are awesome yet practical. This booklet insures his name and wisdom are in print so others can know him and his courage to live the fulness of life.

Passages and thoughts were first shared with close friends in Madison, Wisconsin, July, 2003. This edition has a few more entries to give a more complete picture of Phil's wisdom and perspective on death and the fulness of life. "Fulness" was Phil's preferred spelling.

Entries from Phil's Journals/Notes to Lois contain personal comments. These add to our appreciation of Phil's understanding of fulness of life and death. He often ended a journal entry with the sentiment "Love, ex imo corde" - a Latin phrase meaning "Love - from my innermost heart".

This booklet was assembled by Lois F. Roets. English or Greek or Latin language errors are hers as Phil seldom made an error in any of the 13 languages he could read, write and translate.

Excerpt from Phil's class: Gospel according to John.

Viterbo University, LaCrosse, Wisconsin, Summer, 1967.

Before Jesus was taken, which ultimately led to his death, he was filled with fear and anxiety. He wondered what the father wanted him to do. This was a real human response.

If Adam has not sinned, would there be death? I think "yes" because death is the passage into the fulness of life. The fulness of life is assured by our service to others. We enter the "telos" (Greek word) of our life through death. The fulness of life is "eis telos" - "into the conclusion, fulness, or completeness" by what you have established in life. That fulness is measured by service to others. You can have love of self only if you have served others.

DEATH: A POSITIVE PICTURE.

Whenever a loved one dies, the friends and relatives are filled with sorrow and sadness. The reason is quite simple. Death has taken someone away and there is a sense of emptiness or loss that cannot be replaced. The closer the person was to the people and the more he or she was loved, the deeper the sense of loss will be.

There is one thought that will help to assuage the grief and make sense out of the death. This thought is around us in nature every year of our lives. It is found in the seasons.

If you drive through the country during the winter, the fields are covered with a dry brown or gray grass. The trees are so many seemingly dead branches waving in the air. If you had never seen a field before that winter, you would be convinced it was a barren land.

Drive through the same area at the beginning of spring and you see green starting to come through. Blades of grass or grain are beginning to push their way to the surface. Then walk over to the trees and bushes, and you will see that there are buds on the branches and twigs. The buds look like they are about to burst open.

The sun shines brightly for a few days and the grass and grain grow taller and greener. The buds begin to burst open and show the beginnings of a leaf or blossom. Soon everything will be green and growing again. Spring will work its way into summer. Farmers will work the fields and plant their crops.

Stop by that one farmer. He is planting potatoes. He is dropping small potatoes or pieces of potato into the ground and covering them with dirt. In a few weeks, you see a plant coming up in almost every place a potato was buried. The plant grows. It blossoms and after a few months, the farmer goes out to dig the potatoes. At the bottom of each of those plants there are seven or eight nice, big, new potatoes. Attached to one of the roots of the plant you will find that piece of potato that was dropped into the ground a few months before. It is all dried up and useless.

The little piece of potato or the small potato was dropped into the ground and covered. The new plant sprouted from it and the little piece died in the process. The plant went on to produce the new harvest.

This process of planting the seed in the spring, the seed sprouting new plants, and the hull or shell of the seed shriveling up, the raising of the new crop in the summer, the harvesting in the fall, is the perfect evidence of death and resurrection of every person.

The only difference is that the death of the human being and the resurrection take a bit longer. The undying part of people, the soul or spirit or the inner self, does not die. That part goes on to the place where all people meet. This is called Heaven in the Christian ideas. It is called the Bosom of Abraham in the Jewish picture. Whatever it is called, that is where people go until the world is brought to completion.

At that time there will be a general resurrection of all people and everyone will return to meet all his friends and family and enjoy each other forever.

Death is a separation but not an end to living. The separation is difficult because those who have been left behind have to continue life without that loved one. The comforting thought is that the person who died has gone on to meet other members of the family and is perfectly happy. When the wait on earth is over, you will go to join them.

Death is a positive idea in the same way that planting crops, watching them grow, and harvesting them is a positive process. This process takes place around us every year to give us the assurance that our lives are not empty or wasted. There is a purpose and that purpose is to arrive at the full sharing of life with each other in the ideal home of mankind, heaven.

FINAL IDENTITY: RESURRECTION - BIBLICAL PICTURE

The questions about the life after death or beyond the grave and the resurrection of the whole person at the end of time come up frequently. This was a very difficult point for the first followers of Christ. The apostles and Mary and the other women had first-hand evidence of this resurrection and what it was like. They saw Jesus himself as he appeared and lived among them for forty days. Then he left with the promise of returning after everyone was given an opportunity to choose for or against his teachings.

The notion of the world was limited to the Roman world or empire and all the places were connected by the system of Roman roads. The first Christians thought that the offering of the Good News to the whole world would take only a few years. Everyone would be offered the opportunity to choose for or against. Then would come the "Parousia" or "Second Appearance" of Jesus and the final judgment would take place. All who had chosen Christ would go to live with him and the Father for all eternity in a life of bliss and happiness. All who had chosen against Jesus (his message) would be excluded.

Already with the Thessalonians, in the first letter of Paul, we see a major difficulty on this topic. The people saw their friends and relatives dying. What was going to happen to them at the time of the Parousia? Paul says he does not have the answer for sure. However, he guarantees them that the dead will not lose out. They will be called back and then will come the judgment.

From these practical problems and the proposed answers, the teaching about the resurrection from the dead, the final judgment, and the final lot of happiness was developed. By the time that the written fonts of Revelation were closed with the writings of John, many questions still remained to be answered. Over the years, theologians and churchmen have come up with suggested ideas but no one is sure what this after-life is to be like.

Luke tells us it will be the fulness of salvation. John stresses that it will be an atmosphere of true love for each other.

Matthew says it will be the bringing of everything "eis telos". This Greek phrase means that everything will be brought to its complete fulfillment or perfection. Then, and then only, can we say the plan of Jesus is complete.

What happens to people who deliberately do not live a life in accord with the teachings of Jesus? Jesus says they will be excluded from his presence. They will be cast into the "Valley of Hinnom". In Greek, this is translated as "Gehenna", in Latin as "Infernum", and in English as "Hell".

The meaning is clear. The Valley of Hinnom was a place outside Jerusalem. All the parts of the sacrificial animals that could not be offered in sacrifice, were thrown here. It was a sort of "Temple dump". There was a fire burning there at all times to get rid of the "trash" and remove the stench. Thus the Valley of Hinnom was a place to gather all things that were excluded from the presence of Yahweh in the Temple.

This is the source of many of the notions about "Hell" and "Hellfire" in the later theologies. The main idea that should be stressed is the notion of EXCLUSION. The reason is because the thing or person does not measure up to the required qualities.

A person is given a lifetime to establish his/her identity in the Kingdom of God. At the end of life this identity must be complete. Then for all eternity the person will live and share in the life of God and the saints in keeping with this identity. A person will be able to participate only according to the degree that an identity is established at the moment of death. The only reason for exclusion is that the person is not capable of any participation.

What is the key to this identity? This too, is spelled out in detail. We see it especially in Matthew 28:16-20. The people who are identified are the people who have been kind, understanding and considerate of the people who come into their lives. People who led a life of selfishness and self-centeredness will be excluded.

From one aspect, this identification and salvation are very simple and easy; no big demands are made. From another aspect, this identification is difficult because it involves all the actions of all the days of our lives.

Excerpt from Commentary* on "Book of Wisdom."
* Vol. 2. Commentaries on the Bible: Old Testament and Biblical Themes.

The writer (of Book of Wisdom) treats the problem of people who die young or in their infancy. Where is the love of this God? The writers answer that it is not length of days that gives value to life. Rather, the true value of life comes from the way in which those days are lived. (Wisdom 4:7-14)

Excerpt from Commentary* on "Book of Proverbs"
* Vol.2. Commentaries on the Bible: Old Testament and Biblical Themes.

To become a truly wise person should be the main goal in life for everyone. This goal will demand much persevering effort because it is lifelong. To the very moment of death, a person must be striving to become wise because the most important moment of life is the moment of death. And the most important duty of wisdom is to die wisely. What value does all the rest of your life have if you die "unwisely"?

Excerpt * from "Individual Proverbs and their Applications."
* Vol.2. Commentaries on the Bible: Old Testament and Biblical Themes.

"The virtuous man :: remembered with blessings.
The name of the wicked man :: rots away." Proverbs 10:7.

Life is always expressed in the kind of NAME a person acquires. Sometimes a child has a lot going for him when he gets the name. The parents, grandparents, and other ancestors have made the name known and loved. So the child starts off at the top of the ladder. Other children are not so fortunate. The name they receive has been linked with crime and folly for generations. We often hear that such a child starts off with three strikes against her.

There is some truth in both pictures. However, the name is given to each person. What becomes of that name depends on what the individual does with it in the course of a lifetime. We need only look at some of the heroes in our world to see how true this idea is. Your name at the end of your life will be what you made it. Whether it will live on in fame and blessing or rot away in infamy, depends on what you did with the name in your lifetime. The final value of your name is not what you received but what you did with what you received!

Excerpts from Personal Journals/Notes of Philip G. Roets

Journals/Notes began 6/7/1979 (10th wedding anniversary) to 9/24/2002 (day before he went to hospital and never came home. Phil died in hospital 10/29/02.) The following excerpts apply to death and fulness of life.

May 4, 1980.

It's a beautiful day. I just looked at the freshly cut lawn and all the trees and flowers that seem ready to burst out. Everything has such a rich green color. Each spring we have the season of big dreams and great promises. Then comes the season of heavy work - the summer. Then follows the season of maturing - the fall. Finally comes the season of enjoyment of the promises, goals and work - the winter.

We never attain all the goals set in the spring. We never collect all the promises that were made. But that's why we need another spring. Each year gives us a chance to improve on the last one. Spring, and the following seasons, becomes meaningless only if we get into a rut and do exactly the same thing in exactly the same way each year. Then we fall into the emptiness of monotony.

May 14, 1980.

I (Phil) will not tell you (Lois) not to worry about your parents who are ill. But just recall they have to live their lives and they are to the full. They know your love and appreciation, and they can see the success of their lives all around them.

May 26, 1980. Memorial Day.

On Memorial Day we stop and recall the men and women who believed in this way of life. They believed in it enough that they were willing to fight for it against someone who would destroy it. It is true, wars are destructive foolishness. They add nothing positive to the growth of mankind. But at times force is the only way an aggressor can be stopped. The men and women who died frequently did not believe in war but they did believe in our country and this way of life.

July 1, 1980.

Yesterday I was working on the final verses from the Song of Songs. *"Love is to be worn as a seal on your heart and on your arm. Love is stronger than death and Sheol. The hottest*

10

fire cannot destroy love." The poetic meter in the original Hebrew is beautiful but the ideas are the same in any language. Love must be the source of courage and the motivating force of all action. Love does not end with death nor does it come to a standstill as in the state of suspended animation that was Sheol. Fire can melt even the strongest steel but love it cannot touch.

I like this description because it does tell you some of the strength and quality of my love for you. My love for you is the source of my courage and does motivate my actions.

I watched an older couple in the grocery store. She was in a wheelchair and he was pushing it with one hand and pulling the cart with the other. They were shopping together. She needed him to get around. He needed her to get supplies. Their looks and actions bespoke years of love. This love will not end when one of them dies.

July 27, 1980.
I like the sense of completion I see in the fall. I also always had something new to add to school classes that begin in the fall.

October 21, 1980.
The calendar quotation is from Matthew 25, "If we have lived our lives so that at the end we hear *'Well done, good and faithful servant'* we know that we have not lived in vain." I prefer the checkpoint sooner and more often - that is, every day. What have I accomplished for the day that is of lasting value for me and those with whom I live? This makes life worth living.

There is a difference between enjoyment and fun. Enjoyment is the sense of deep, personal satisfaction that comes of success in the use of your abilities. Enjoyment depends primarily on self. Fun is dependent on other people or things. Fun is good but fleeting. Enjoyment is enduring and perfective of the doer.

November 1, 1980.
There are lots of problems and they do cause anxiety and discouragement at times. But I firmly believe the minds of people are big enough to cope with any problem if we can develop the leaders.

January 9, 1981.

I am convinced that I as this person do not cease to exist at death. I don't know how I continue but I am convinced that I shall continue to be myself in some way. The goal of my life more than ever is to establish peace, understanding, friendship, sympathy, tolerance, patience, ambition and enthusiasm for myself and those with whom I come into contact.

January 11, 1981.

Last night, you asked if I would talk with you about the notion of after-life. I think we continue to exist and continue to know each other in some way. First of all, I think it is quite well established that energy once created is not lost. It is converted into other forms and continues on. The human brain is constantly putting out energy. The highest form of this energy is from the cerebrum in which we have knowledge, memory, and especially self-awareness, and the ability to communicate this self-awareness to others.

This brain is a part of our physical inheritance and so is constantly related to those from whom we come. So I believe or feel we will continue to live in union with our loved ones and continue to develop. The pace or speed of this development will always be primarily up to us. Environment will have some part to play in it.

Thus I think the message of the Jews and the Christians has much validity. We receive our talents or abilities and the opportunity to develop them. If we sincerely work at this we will be happy. If we fail through laziness, lack of initiative or wastefulness, we will be frustrated and unhappy.

So to sum it up, I am convinced the more we develop and grow in this life, the more we will be able to continue on when the stage called death is reached. I see death as the planting of a seed. The seed is never destroyed if it sprouts and sends out a shoot. The seed is very much alive in the new plant and fruit.

This, I think, is the meaning of the Biblical Greek term "synteleia" in which all things are continuously brought together to establish the home of mankind.

I love you, Sweetie. When I say it is eternal, this is what I mean. It will never die. And each new growth of love makes it that much more potent and enduring.

January 12, 1981.

Yesterday and this morning, I have been doing a lot of thinking about the after-life since you brought the question up to me. Rather, I mentioned the point and you asked for my explanation.

I think my ideas are exactly the same as they were fifteen or twenty years ago. Creation or the universe is an ongoing event. It is a very orderly process as we are learning more and more. So it would seem to me there is a very definite plan. The goal is a constant evolving upward to a more and more perfect life. The human stage we have reached now is seemingly the first in which there is a keen self-awareness as a person. This gives rise to the ability and need to communicate with others and to cooperate in living. It also fails in the overstress of self which is selfishness and thus self-destructive.

Our lives now are the developing of our true selves: thinking, creating, sharing, cooperating, and helping each other. All this is bound together in various degrees and stages of love. This self-awareness or self-existence has to continue after death, otherwise the evolving or creative process has fallen backwards in its highest development. This has not happened before. So I think some kind of true after-life, sharing and loving are demanded.

Where, how, when -- are all questions that have yet to be answered just as so many unanswered questions have been suddenly answered in the last two decades.

We're building for our future together. It's a great "savings plan" or "salvation plan" as theology called it.

January 27, 1981.

Difficulties to be overcome can either strengthen the will to succeed or destroy it. A person can overcome the difficulty or be overcome by it.

There is no such thing as a life without difficulty. The obstacle may seem simple or meaningless to someone else but it is very real to the one facing it. Climbing a steep hill is always work but it's really fun to look from the top of the hill to the whole area around. If a person climbs to the top and then spends all his time looking down and thinking how tough it was, the climb has been mostly a waste. If he looks out and enjoys what he has attained he has real success.

February 4, 1981.
We are certainly used to adjustments. We've made many in our personal lives, religious life, and in our marriage. We will have more adjustments to make.

We'll pull along together.
Our love binds our cooperation;
Our sincerity smooths out the rough patches.

March 19, 1981.
Good morning! The feast of St. Joseph. I am quite sure I commented on this great man. But I'll do it again.

Very often in the past few months I have called on Joseph for help. As I have said, I am firmly convinced that life here on earth is not the end of all things. To say that a person is just "snuffed out" at death seems to make everything futile and meaningless.

We certainly continue on in our words and the people we have influenced by our lives. But I don't think that is enough either. I believe, but I cannot explain, that great people - like Joseph and all good-living people - still exist in the same way. They are happy and they are able to help us in some way. I think this is what was meant by heaven in the Jewish-Christian tradition. If a person's life is empty and unproductive, then that person has no further identity at death. This is hell in the same tradition. The same emptiness is theirs forever.

As I say I cannot prove these ideas. I think I can show this is what was believed and taught by the first Christians. I don't think we have gone beyond these ideas, nor have we come up with something better.

So I have talked to Joseph and Mary and Jesus many many times. I have felt a real strength and courage and calmness as a result.

Joseph faced the difficulty of hard times; a gifted child who was a challenge to raise; a minority group who was oppressed; being uprooted because of political upheaval; and the problems connected with a small, tightly interwoven social structure. For his greatest support he had a loving, understanding, helpful wife and other children.

14

April 12, 1981.

You asked about my thoughts on after life. I am told that energy, once set in motion, is never lost. It is converted again and again but is constantly used. To me the greatest evidence is the piece of coal or wood or food. The solar and mineral energy has combined to store the heat energy. Millions of years or seasons later, that heat energy is released by burning or by digestion. It warms me or it nourishes me.

The greatest or highest form of energy output we know is from the human brain. Whether we call it spiritual with the Greeks, or intellectual with the Scholastics, or cerebral with the scientist doesn't make a particle of difference. The energy is produced. It remains. It is used over and over. It is identified with me and gives me identity. This identity remains and I think goes on existing and perfecting as my person. This continuing identity I call an after-life or an eternal life.

How this is to be accomplished is still a puzzle to us. But I don't consider that an obstacle. If someone had talked of an airplane to the people on the Oregon Trail, they would all have enjoyed it but no one would have taken it seriously. Airplanes were impossible then and up to 1903. Yet we now have shuttles going to outer space.

Flying was just as much a possibility in the time of DaVinci as it was to the Wright Brothers. Space travel was just as feasible in the days of Jules Verne as it was in the time of John F. Kennedy. DaVinci was considered an idle dreamer; Verne was a fiction writer with unlimited imagination. The reality of flying and space travel matched the human dream almost to the letter.

I think the same thing will happen with life after death. The formula will be unlocked and people will share their identities. This will be the "hell of it". If a person has not established a lasting identity, there will be nothing to share. It will be like going to the AERA (American Educator's Research Association) conference to mingle with great creative scholarly people and all you have done is work on frivolous interests.

August 17, 1981.

Last night you asked about my belief in a heaven or after-life. Again I have thought much about this in recent months and especially in reference to the term "Kingdom". Mt. 25:31-46 is the climax of the development of kingdom in that gospel account. It is often referred to as the judgment scene. I prefer the term " self-identification" scene.

First of all, it is a universal scene - everybody is included. Then Jesus is referred to first as the Son of Man. This is his act as the human being! In the next sentence he is called the "King" and God is the "Father". The picture described is the firm, final and eternal establishment of the brotherhood of man in the fatherhood of God. Verse 34 is the one that always catches my attention. *"Welcome, people happy in your Father.*
Accept as your inheritance,
the kingship prepared for you
from the foundation of the world."

This time of fulfillment is at hand. Everyone who is being addressed is a fully identified member of the family of man in the fatherhood of God. Each is a first class member of the family and therefore receives an inheritance. The inheritance means it is not a free gift but is theirs by right as member of the family. This inheritance is the kingship which was described already in the creation picture of Genesis. This kingship is the control and correct use of the world about us in peace, harmony, happiness and success. This inheritance will be divided in strict justice according to the merits of each in the use of higher talents in daily life.

Then comes the really consoling part. Christ is talking. He says, I was hungry, thirsty, naked, stranger, sick and in prison -- and you cared for my needs. Christ as the first-born in the family identifies all the brothers and sisters with himself. Thus the family of mankind is being established.

Heaven will be the full enjoyment and continued living in this human family. The other side of the picture is the emptiness, waste, and frustration of not belonging simply because a person did not use the opportunities offered.

Where will this heaven be? I think it will be the re-people of this earth as it is brought to perfection. In the meantime I think that the people already dead are enjoying this happiness in anticipation of what is to come.

The justice is not a matter of books and accounts. The

justice is the person each one has become. No one can take away or add to your personality. This you create and it is totally yours. The creation is the visible fruit of love.

January 26, 1982.
When I awoke this morning my first thought was in part of our conversation of last night. What is the after-life? Or, what will it be like after death?

I had just been reading on this question in 1st Corinthians 15. This whole chapter deals with resurrection and after life. One of the explicit questions is: What will it be like? Paul, or in this part of the letter Luke, who edited Paul's writings, answers: *"We don't know. Look at the seed put into the ground. Who could guess the plant or the tree or the flower or the fruit that would come from it?"* I really like this answer. If the initial egg and sperm cell are able to contain all the genes that develop into me and my talents, I cannot see such a wise orderly plan going "poof" into nothingness at the moment of death.

I like the New Testament term for death - "palingenesis" Greek word for "a rebirth". We start over from where we are at that moment of development to become a more complete or perfect being. The one difference is that it is no longer a period of testing but a period of fulness and arrival.

In Second Timothy, Paul uses three comparisons: 1) the athlete who has played hard and is now a recognized pro in the Hall of Fame; 2) a soldier who has fought hard but now the battle is won; 3) a farmer who has worked and toiled but now the harvest is gathered into the barn and he can enjoy the fruits of his labors. However he starts to plan for next year.

I think this question and these attempted answers are the heart of human living.

October 26, 1982.
It surprises me but the older I get the less I am worried about what happens after I die. I feel I am following my conscience sincerely. I hurt people's feelings at times but it is seldom out of meanness. I am quick to recognize the failure and admit and sincerely want to do something to atone. So I feel I can live at peace with myself and that's all I can do.

I feel we are closer to each other with each passing year.

We will never have a passive or dull existence because we both have strong opinions and ideas of what we want. But I feel we have the kind of love that brings true harmony out of this struggling. In short, we write the symphony of our lives which does not die any more than the symphonies of Beethoven.

December 19, 1982.

As I look out on the world of winter, I see a time of fulfillment and a time of promise; a time of challenge and a time of security; a time to be treasured and a time to be used.

My love is fulfillment, challenge, security, treasure, is you.

January 4, 1983. (Lois's dad was ill)

I woke up completely at 4:20 so I got up. I've thought a lot about our discussion of your Dad, last night, and I'll try to get a few of my ideas on paper.

At the homes for the elderly in Oconomowoc, Watertown and Mount Calvary (Wisconsin), I visited and worked with hundreds of people each week. Many of them were farm people from those areas. Most of them were in there 80's. Some few were upset, miserable and could not be calmed or comforted. The vast majority had this calm sort of distant look much of the time. They were not out of contact with reality. I always felt they were seeing reality - the reality of their lives fully and with lengthy hindsight and deep foresight.

Experience comforted them as they saw all they had accomplished. They could talk about hardships and difficulties almost with a note of endearment, certainly with pride. They still did not like the hardship but they could see clearly how they had succeeded in the face of difficulty and success was sweet.

Their foresight looked ahead. They did not know what was there but they had the strong conviction that nothing good was ever lost and they themselves would continue in some way to enjoy it. They were never sad as if they were leaving. Instead they seemed convinced this was but the first stage in real or lasting community with those they always loved.

I have always felt we should concentrate on all the good days and times and events we had with those we loved. We all know we have not been perfect. Many events we would like to change. We can't. So we go with the ones that succeeded.

I saw many many Redemptorists (CSsR) grow old and die. So many of these had a difficult time with both. So many complained day after day. Then I watched great men like Fathers Ben Lenz and Ed Fastner, Brother Angelo. These men lived and died happy and content because they succeeded in spite of the structure. I was confessor and adviser for years to the older nuns at Elm Grove, WI. Week after week I saw these people rich in the memories of people they had helped and taught and formed. They too died happy.

I like this old adage: "The evil that men do is quickly forgotten; the good lives on forever." In fact, that is what evil is: it **isn't**. Evil is a lack of something that should have been. It is non-existent.

I hope these words are some comfort and help.

January 5, 1983.

Death is always one of the major stress points of life. As we have both said and heard so often, it is far more important to be concerned with how you live than how you die. Living lasts for years but dying is only a few hours. Living is the way to prepare to die.

That thought can sound so morbid and yet it is a core truth. The real significance of life is how you establish an identity that never dies. This is certainly done in the people with whom and for whom you live. But I firmly believe it is done in some personal way that never ends.

Just as energy is never lost, so I believe that the source of human energy that is "me" continues on in my personal identity in some way.

I love you, Sweetie! I'll help you in any way I can. My love for you gives all my actions a meaning that is satisfying and rewarding in a way I never imagined.

January 6, 1983.

I'll pick up a point of our discussion from last night. You said your mom sounded a bit hurt at the conduct of your Dad. I saw this in working with older married couples very often. Frequently, I was tempted to say something but I seldom ever did. I figured when a couple had lived together for 40, 50, 60 years, there had to be a solid love in both of them. They had faced many a problem together and succeeded. They had many a difference of opinions and both learned to cope with the situation. Most of the time they were able to filter out the hurt or the disagreeable and see only the good parts of the events.

Then, too, people in there eighties are not judging events by what they still have to do. They have lots of work planned but there is always the proviso that they may not be able to get it done. Experience, aging, and need have taught them a realistic approach to potential. As long as people like your Mom have a sounding board and sympathetic ear they get along fine.

December 31, 1983.

I am firmly convinced of the key work of my life: I have to make myself. I am self-made as is every person. When I come to the end of my life, all that I'll have is the person I've made. I don't know whether the person continues to exist or dies with the mortal death. I am not really concerned about that. All I know is I have to be pleased with the self I am becoming or nobody will be pleased. My basic self I like. I have weaknesses but I have a lot of strengths. These strengths are the points I concentrate on.

April 10, 1984.

You asked me what feelings I have when I hear that men like Bill and Ty (priests and friends of Phil from Milwaukee) are gone. I suppose it is just the inevitability of death. In my adult life, I have talked to dying people so many times and have discussed and preached about death so often that I have very positive convictions about it.

I have always felt that death will be a satisfying part of life if you are content with the person you have made yourself to be.

I am firmly convinced that people do not cease to be. I firmly believe that people like (Fathers) Bill Loesch and Lenz, and all the others who really spent their lives in the service of others, live on in some way to enjoy the personality they have created. Such a belief is a part of every known tradition of human thought. We do not know how this takes place any more than we know what is contained in outer space. We are evolving in the extent of our knowledge. As you say, research and leadership are the focal points of education and life.

April 20, 1984.

I think the part of the Christian ideal that always appealed to me is that life is love, love is service, and service is a day-by-day, action-by-action living with and for others.

This life creates me - the person I want to be, and that person will not be annihilated. What happens to me or how it happens I don't know and I don't really care. I am just sure that great people like Loesch & Kolanko (priests in Milwaukee area) and you will never cease to be.

I've known lots of people in my years. I've worked with and for lots of them. I was always noted for giving the extra hour or two of work. I was appointed to thousands of jobs simply because the superiors knew they would be done. But I made a point always to take personal pride in what I was doing - whether that was cleaning the toilets, cutting trees, plowing snow, tutoring other students, teaching, or whatever. And it always paid off. I felt good about what I did even when it was not noticed.

You (Lois) are the one person in my life whom I love fully. My expression of that love is still much the same "service". But this love is unique. I'm sorry it cannot alleviate all your aches and pains and mental anguish but I want to.

May 18-19, 1984.

A person must have roots, wings and memories. The roots will give us an identity and sense of personal worth. The wings will give support to ambitions. And the memories are what remain for all times.

The interaction with others and events causes or makes memories. That is what is left of you after the events are gone. Our continued existence is primarily the way in which we live on in the lives of others. Whether there is anything more than that remains to be seen. But we do know and can see how others live in us and how we already live in them.

September 4, 1984.

There is no clear explanation for sickness, evil or death except that they are built into the system and are the other side of the coin.

March 24, 1985.

Yesterday, as I was working on the summaries of the Old Testament, the role of God in the stories of people took on a new dimension for me. I'm sure I heard it often before but it finally registered for me: God is someone or something that is personally attractive to this individual. "To be with God" means to attain perfect happiness as this person views it. Hence the Indians talked about the Great Spirit in the Happy Hunting Ground. The Biblical people saw it as the family of Abraham in perfect harmony with each other and excluding all gentiles. The Christians extended the idea to the whole of mankind.

Today, then, we should be concentrating on what would make for true and lasting happiness for the individual. In this sense everyone has to create his or her own God. But because we are social beings this God will have to be someone or something that fits into our social awareness.

In this sense, the two phrases of the New Testament that seem to be readily appropriate are: "God is Spirit" and "God is Love". He/she/it is the spirit of any person or group as it impels them to action. God is love insofar as this spirit must spring from love and create greater love.

Thus it seems to me that I can weave the writing I was doing yesterday and the work on Spirit into a unit. At least it is a step closer to my thinking.

Oct 29, 1985.

There is no way of measuring the lives we have made greater because of our work in the classroom. Where does the influence end?

Look at nature. The seeds of one generation are not only the source of the next but the more scientists learn of genetics, the more they know the strengths and weaknesses can be carried forward.

Now put this on an intellectual and emotional level. These too are carried on and recognized.

I think the time comes when this consciousness reaches full maturity, when we become aware of all the people who have made us, and share with them in some continued life. Nature is constantly evolving and we are part of that nature. When we develop far enough we'll see the connections. Nothing is lost but takes a while to unfold.

All this becomes clearer to me, not because of some special revelation, but because of the nature of the world of which we are living parts.

November 21, 1985.

Now to pick up our conversation of last evening. First of all, I think there is one major danger of being a "mover and shaker" in any organization. Those in charge quickly take your work for granted. They don't have to bother their heads about you. The parents don't complain and the students like you. So, every once and awhile, this being overlooked, or worse "trod on" hurts deeply. Then it's time to rile the waters so they know you are a vital person.

I feel I went through this type of life in my seminary days and all my life as a priest. At every stage, I had one person I could spout off to when I needed: (Fathers) Joe Flanagan, John Zeller, Benny Lenz, Bill Loesch. I frequently listened to their spoutings in return.

I often wonder if the whale is a good analogy. The whale blows and gets rid of its used air and takes in a new supply. However, that is also its most vulnerable moment.

December 23, 1985.

Event: a difficult situation over which we had little influence.
I (Phil) won't let myself get bitter because I could ruin the rest of my life and ours. We'll continue to live our lives as we see fit.

February 9, 1986.

Wayne (Phil's brother-in-law, husband of his sister in Kansas) has brought up all the questions of the "whys" and "wherefores" of living and dying. I never dig too deeply into them because I find my reasons for living in the immediate job I am doing. I never did have an answer for dying and I still don't. Everyone else has died and no one has ever returned to tell us about it. So I figure I'll make the best of it when my turn comes.

August 8, 1986.

I want to jot down the statement at your Uncle Henry's funeral:

"You people have gathered here not because Henry Schelle died but because he lived among you." That is the fullest and richest encomium of praise I have ever heard in so few words.

October 1, 1986. Topic: Change and optimism.

You (Lois) asked if everything would turn out rightly and my answer is an unequivocal and optimistic "yes". We have to face new issues constantly but we have a pattern of success in the unusual. The place changes, the work changes, people change, you and I change. This is the basic fact of all life. It's up to us to make the changes into improvements. This is the challenge of change. We can improve anything together. We have the safety and security of our home as a place to recoup and recap. Then we can sally forth to our victories.

The best is yet to come even though it seems hard to prove at times.

Oct 3, 1986.

Everything will come to a good end with a few setbacks in between. That's life and we've lived through it often.

January 1, 1987.

Happiness - Creative Growth;
Productivity - Serenity;
Excited Expectation - Love, Contentment.

These goals are what I'd like to accomplish in 1987. I'd like to attain all these in proper proportions throughout the year for us both. I don't say "receive" because I don't want them as a gift. I want to earn them by my own actions.

January 6, 1987.

Last night, you were talking about your Dad's health. From working around older people for years, the one adjective I can say fits all of them is "unpredictable". Just as the body builds up in varied ways, so it wears down in varied ways.

He certainly lived a full life, left his mark on the world in which he lived, and can die content. Just as no form of energy is ever lost in nature, so I don't think any form of man's life is lost. Since conscious life is the greatest part of this life, and sharing with others is the greatest part of consciousness, I think these will continue is some form not known to us. I have no evidence for it. I just think it follows the laws of the world in which we live.

May 1, 1987.
I can't say much when you talk about your Dad. I'll listen. I'll suffer with you. But you have to get the picture into focus. I suggest you concentrate on all the good memories because these are your real Dad (not the dad who is in the nursing home).

May 11, 1987.
Your Dad's body is wearing out but his personality, which we all saw for so many years, will never die. That personality is intimately bound up with his family. That personality will meet you again. You call it the next life, eternal life, metamorphosis, or whatever explanation is put forth. It will come and you will enjoy it.

May 31, 1987.
Your dad is no longer physically at home (he's in nursing home) and in his mind he has only fleeting recognition of himself and others. I would advise that you think much of what you gave your folks during their golden years. You gave your Mom the little vacuum that she used so much. We gave them their first colored TV set; many gifts of cheese and crackers which they enjoyed but would never buy for themselves; a trip through parts of Canada, New York, Washington DC and much of the east; trips to South Dakota, Kansas, Oklahoma and states in-between. These trips were leisurely times and your folks could enjoy the whole of it. You've talked with both your dad and mom many times and helped them see through questions or difficulties. Your parents are truly grateful to you.

July 23, 1987.
As for life hereafter or some sort of continuance in being, I feel sure each person continues to enjoy what he/she has made self to be. I don't know how because it is the next stage of life.

December 11, 1987.

I'm sorry to hear of your Mom's suffering. I surely do not know the cause although as you say, she really wore herself out physically, emotionally and nervously in trying to care for your Dad at home and now to look after his care in the nursing home. This could be the reaction her body is putting forth in reaction to the stress. It is certainly not fair but your Mom has learned to cope with this aspect of life long ago.

People have tried to develop philosophies and religions to explain the incongruities, inconsistencies, and unfairness of life. Everyone has come up short in some or many circumstances.

Many have tried the Happy Hunting Ground, Nirvana, Heaven, Pie-in-the-Sky for the future. Others have given the theory of sin and punishment. Others feel it is lack of faith. None of the systems ever answers the basic question: Why does the person who tries hard and gives wholeheartedly get bowled over and kicked, and the self-centered egotistical bastard comes out on top? Violence is not the answer. Yet law and order don't cope. Meekness and turning the other cheek just means more bruises and a silly grin.

Have a good day. I'll do what I can to make our world better for the day. My love is yours totally.

March 29, 1988.

In the seminary, we had a long treatment of the notion of evil in philosophy and theology. The question of an all-good God permitting the just to suffer all the evil unjustly never proved a sticker for me. I never saw God as all good. The depiction of the deities by the pagans had much evil even in their good gods. The Old Testament always presented Yahweh as a very vengeful God if people did not follow his plan. The Apocalyptic tradition in the last century BC gave us "Satan" or the "Adversary". The Gospel writers developed this notion of God as Father, and Satan as the rebelling angel, and then the theologians developed a demon to cover every possibility. I read all this stuff, admired the ingenuity and imaginative opportuneness of the proponents, and then wrote it off as a huge and intricate mental structure, set on a side hill, with a foundation of ten feet of foam.

June 20, 1988 .

I enjoyed our discussion of the Joannine (writings of John) ideas of life and death, last night. The crudity and barbarity of the fertility rites of Roman times always appalled and disgusted me. The Apocalyptic writers of the Old Testament, starting with Ezechial, began to write against them.

Then the synoptic gospels (Matthew, Mark, Luke) offered the various aspects of the Kingdom of Heaven as the counteraction. Finally by 125 A.D., the Joannine writer was able to take the analogies of life and death: seed, plant and fruit, death and renewal, and show how all of these were to be established in this life by sincere respect and love the people had for each other. They shared in their community or family meals. I think the "ritual" as seen in John was that every meal (evening) was to be an expression of "koinonia" (Greek word for "sharing") as the Passover had been for the Jews. The Christian life would then change death into life as Christ had done by his willingness to live and die for his ideals.

This, I think, is the essence of Christian ideals. It is a philosophy of life with no community larger than the local one, no ritual other than a family meal or a potluck supper, and no organization other than the world about them. This would become "the eternal life" narrated by John -- the life that would last forever.

July 4, 1988.

I never cease to wonder about a scholar like Joseph Campbell. He works with and translates Sanskrit and yet when it comes to many of the basic Biblical ideas he takes them from the catechism or a theology book of the 13th century.

He was particularly interested in the final aspect of the world and people. So he quotes from the catechism meaning of the text. "To Telos" means "end" in the sense of fulfillment or fulness. When I look at the two tea jars on our deck, I see them in the process of brewing tea. Some time today, according to your decision, they will reach their "telos" - their purpose or fulness. At that time, the jars will be filled with brewed tea and you can drink it as you will. In no way will the jars have been destroyed or ruined.

Matthew goes a step farther in this development of this

notion in his summary of the Gospel story in the last 3 verses of the Gospel (MT 28:26-28) "Go forth: Make disciples of all nations. Behold: 'I am' in your midst until the end of the world."

The Christians are not to be isolated people like the Jews (who were in small isolated groups). They are to go everywhere. They are not to live in ghettoes but to mingle with everyone and bring about "the perfect and harmonious working together of everything in the world." This perfect harmony is "I am" or the divine presence which the Jews sought.

All this would be readily understandable to Matthew's readers: The Jewish Christians. It had to be explained and applied to John's Gentile readers. He calls it "Love 'eis telos' " (chapters 13-17). Not one single word of this is found in the catechism or the theologians. They all worked from a Latin translation "finis" and developed "end" in the sense of annihilation and destruction. With this initial mistranslation in vogue, they could devote a whole volume to "de ultimus" or "the last things" - that is, what would happen at the end of the world.

Gradually, this aspect of Christian theology smothered out the common sense of the original New Testament picture. We ended with the mountebanks preaching hell, damnation, vengeance, vindictive justice and the like.

The League of Nations and the United Nations would be good examples of "synteleia"* on paper. The problem is to put them into action.

* "Synteleia" is Greek word for "completion, fulness".

January 13-14, 1989.

A huge world of events has taken place since I wrote the last note forty-eight hours ago. We have discussed many aspects of your Dad over the years I have known him. His niche in the world is secured forever. He died as he had lived - a breath at a time. He took his last breath and calmly relaxed into eternity.

It is true we have no idea what he is doing or where he is but of one thing I am sure: the fulness of his life and person can never just disappear. No matter what you call it, your Dad has gone to join the others that preceded him in an eternal abode: heaven, happy-hunting-ground, Nirvana - whatever. He is there and can enjoy the fruit of a full life. The body that was his temporary home wore out and he left that behind. We will bury that body on Monday. It is venerated and respected like a former home but it is put aside. Your Dad in his real self lives on. We should now stress the "life" and "reward" and "pleroma" (Greek word for "fulness") or fulness promised.

You talk often of being able to feel contact with others at a distance. After the initial pain of loss is overcome, you can develop the life of new closeness and strength with your Dad. You don't need a medium or a seance. The contact is there for the taking if it was built initially in this life - and it was.

January 15-19, 1989.

Your Dad died a peaceful death surrounded by his family. All the ravages of sickness, age and death were removed and he was presented for that final viewing as the handsome, well-groomed man that he was. People of all ages walked past him to seal their final memory of the man they knew, loved, respected, admired and imitated. The funeral dinner was by way of a banquet celebration. Everyone could look over the crowd and see at a glance that the Schelle & Goecke (Lois's parents) alliance would go forward in stalwart representation. Your mom did a marvelous job of taking the chair of honor to continue her role as matriarch.

After the funeral and dinner and guests had departed, there was a family meeting. Your Mom can carry on with the goals she and Charles (Lois's dad) had begun. Now it is up to Charlie's descendants to prove they are truly heirs of his estate- not just his property - but his ideals, his ambition, effort, consideration, love, and his successes. I have no doubt Charlie knows what we are doing but we have to wait our turn to see what he is doing. It's like a one-way window.

March 17, 1989.

I don't think it's surprising that you feel overwhelmed once in awhile.

You have accumulated many "stress points" in less than a year: change of jobs, moving to another home, bought a new home, food poisoning at a meeting, my retirement (Phil's), and your dad's final sickness and death. It will always be one individual event or person that triggers the reaction. In this case it was the little first grader and his trying to fathom the injustice of death of a loved one. Great minds, adult minds, have been baffled by the question since the beginning of time. They built up all sorts of rites, rituals and symbols to offset or palliate the stark reality. This little boy has only his anger and self-inflected pain demanded by frustration. As you said, it's good the mother asked for help.

I love you, Sweetie. I am in full sympathy with you. We've weathered big problems together before. I'm sure we can surmount this mountain. My love and support are all yours.

May 29, 1989. Topic: Power of Love.

The more we talk about the meaning, value and power of love, the more I see the dynamic force of love as portrayed in the Gospel and how the notion was emasculated over the centuries.

Love is an active giving, an active receiving, and a mutually active give and take from that initial exchange. As soon as either party takes the active exchange out of love, it loses its force.

This is why handouts achieve nothing. There is no active receiving. This is what debilitates the welfare state. This is what destroys the power of so-called philanthropy. The Gospel story is bound up in the word "love" but it is a living, responsible force.

July 29, 1989. Topics: changing times, unique persons, and "fulness of life".

The newspaper says that girl athletes have now added chewing tobacco to their list of achievements.

The only woman I ever saw chew tobacco was Mrs. Smith in Derby, Kansas. She was the age of Grandma Roets. Her husband was dead and her three children lived on the west coast. According to Grandma Roets, Mrs. Smith was a wonderful neighbor. She smoked cigars, a pipe, and chewed tobacco - but only at home. We went to visit her with Grandma on several occasions. I took a fiendish delight in watching her smoke a pipe or chew tobacco and use the spittoon. She made excellent cookies and was extremely generous with them.

Additional Information: Phil really liked cookies. Therefore, people who made good cookies and shared them generously with Phil were wonderful "good and fine" people. Cookies, and a meal shared in friendship, were definitely a part of Phil's "fulness of life ".

August 27, 1989. Topic: Phil observed, enjoyed, and respected nature.

When I moved the box of twigs and grass clippings, I found 18 huge night crawlers on the cement under the leaves. I'm sure they crawled out of their holes to avoid drowning and got under the leaves where it was moist and safe. I put all of them back on the grass and left it up to their ingenuity to get in the soil again.

August 31, 1989.
> Topic: Forgiveness in daily events. Phil said you had to ask forgiveness
> of the one offended before any forgiveness could be given by others.

I'm sorry I sounded like a bear with his ass in a steel trap last night. I was disgusted with the tutoring* and had not resolved the issues in my own mind. I should have kept quiet until I saw the light at the end of the tunnel.

> *Explanation of the situation: Tutoring Service kept changing Phil's
> schedule - at the last minute. The students being tutored were fine.

September 15, 1989. Topic: The Seasons.

Spring is always a sense of awakening and coming back to life after a time of cold, snow, frost and ice. It's wonderful to see the rich green take over the drab browns and grays of winter. There is also an urgency for the work that has to begin.

Fall, to me, is a sense of expectancy that comes from the gathering. The reward of labor is being brought in. There is an air of getting ready to rest and enjoy what has been earned or made. The flowers and plants of spring look fine and brittle. The flowers and plants of fall look strong and worn and productive.

The changing of the seasons is a sign of the mobility of nature and the stability of the plan.

November 3, 1989.

I'll be at the airport to meet and greet you today. (Lois was at the National Association for Gifted Children conference). It will be very nice to have you home again. I can keep myself busy all during the day. That's not much different from a regular workday. I really miss you in the morning in our beginning exchanges of the day, and then again at night when we sit and talk. Taking a bath and hiking to bed seem like such empty chores compared with when you are home. Welcome back - my love!

January 13, 1990.

It seems almost impossible that a whole year has passed since your Dad died. I woke up this morning, thinking about your Dad and the value of life. You speak at times of loss of hope and yet your Dad is one of the greatest symbols of hope you can find. He grew up on the edge of a tiny town. He lived and farmed in this tiny spot for all his adult years. He retired and moved into town and continued his hobby of woodworking. Your Mom was his partner in all his adult years.

From his life as a farmer, he gave the world a scientific advance in the development of seed corn. He studied and applied new ways of scientific farming. He worked long, hard hours and left his mark on the world. That mark spreads throughout many states of the nation. Through your work (Lois), the influence of your dad and mom is spread through your books throughout all the world in the education of gifted children.

Yes, there is reason for hope because good people die and their heritage lives on after them.

At work, you can't make a change that is not challenged. I think of it as your Dad cultivating his corn. He prided himself on keeping the weeds out of the field. But he never figured he had killed the weeds once and for all. Each year they came again, and each year he cultivated row after row to get the weeds out and keep the moisture in. That's hope! You never finish but the field is always better after you get finished.

March 17, 1990. Event: Pauline Lohkamp Roets, Philip's Mother, died.

I believe a person goes on to whatever comes after this life. The person is whatever he or she has made of self in the course of this life. Saint Ambrose (4th century, A.D.) described life and death centuries ago, in a way that always appealed to me. He said a person is born into this life with a certain amount of ability. Life and life's events are the time and occasions to develop your person into the self you want to be. When death comes you will be able to receive the amount of fulness or completion that you have developed the capacity for. I adapted Ambrose's ideas to the making of a wagon. The size, kind, and capacity are the work of a lifetime. At death, that wagon will be filled to capacity according to my making. Every wagon will be full but the amount depends on the size of the wagon. Mom's wagon will be full whatever its size.

Since I've known you, my wagon has grown immensely in quality, size and value. My love and support are yours always.

P.s. Happy St. Patrick's Day! He came from Spain and
was probably a Basque shepherd.

March 18, 1990.
I've lived my life as I saw fit. My life has been a life of service to others and it is still that. I have given direction, impetus and meaning to the lives of many. I reach a lot of people through my teaching, published writings and audiotapes, and newspaper columns in the <u>Herald</u>. (twice-weekly columns 1982-1994). All this gives me satisfaction and a sense of purpose. I've made a lot of big decisions in my 68 years. The most important and best was the decision to team up with you.

March 21, 1990.
I've led a life of service to others and I'm happy with what I've done, am doing, and will do.

September 25, 1990.
I've worked hard all my life and done a great amount in the service of others. I still have a lot of ideas to share with people and will continue to do so by writing. I believe firmly in the Christian ethic but not in the emasculated farce developed by some theologians and churchmen.

October 13, 1990.
You (Lois) made a statement that my notion of my personal worth lay in my service to others. That's not quite the whole picture as I see it. I know my own intrinsic value. I know the talents I have and the way I have worked to develop them. I use these abilities for others and myself. If other people appreciate what I do, I enjoy that. At the same time, I will not let myself be taken or used by some "smartass". I can hold my tongue if I think it's the right thing to do, but I can and do tell off anyone who tries to "use" me.

I enjoy being with people but I also can spend many

hours alone reading or writing or in manual work. I enjoy just plain looking - to see events or to observe nature.

November 26, 1990.
As for legacy - I've left a big one among people for 42 years. I'll continue the articles in the newspaper and I'll work on the Biblical commentaries. For me, that is enough. I've led a life of service. The people I've served have benefited from my help and most of them gave me recognition while I could still receive it. One "thank you" while I am alive is worth much more to me than a huge bouquet of flowers on my coffin. I couldn't smell them.

> Additional Information: Phil taught at Upper Iowa University -
> Des Moines campus, from 1989 - 1994: Spanish I & II,
> Business Ethics, Intro to Philosophy, Philosophy of Religion.

January 16, 1991.
I did a lot of thinking during the night. My question was always the same: What is the legacy I leave? I started out years ago on the advice of Joe Flanagan and John Zeller (priests in the seminary whom Phil liked and whose opinions Phil valued) to let my legacy be written in the people I serve. I have done this all through the years. Most of the people may not even remember my name but the influence I had on their lives is still going on. I see this in the lives of all priests and religious whose lives I influenced for my 22 years as a priest. The majority in every group were helped toward fulness of faith and life. I've done it in the lives of almost all the kids and adults I've taught. That is the legacy I want to leave and am leaving.

What do I owe you (to Lois, his wife)? If you want a day by day picture, you'll have to go back through these journal books. You gave me new drive and zest. I can't imagine my life without you in the center. I try to repay this a tiny bit by my attention and service.

I never intentionally hurt you. I go against the grain at times, I know, but I also know that's part of nature.

April 15, 1991. Topics: It's nice to be remembered; simple things make us happy.
Thank you for the Itsy Bitzy Montana Yo-Yo. (Lois was conducting workshops for educators in Montana.) Yo-yos were the rage when I was in grade school. Some of them could do almost

unbelievable tricks. I could never afford one so I made my own. I took two Tinker Toys and fastened them together with one of the tiny sticks. I attached the string on the inside and then I painted stripes on it. At first, other kids laughed at it and then they were asking to try it. It didn't take on as a great invention but I had hours of fun from it. At the end of my first year at Kirkwood (minor seminary near St. Louis), I won some footraces. One of the prizes was a yo-yo and I got it.

July 26, 1991.

I am reminded of our discussion on life and its meaning. I think I have clarified a notion for myself. I think life is a continuous gift. It has a beginning but no end.

There are three stages: The **Genesis:** This is the act of receiving life or being born onto this earth. Then comes the years of **Becoming:** the years of identifying ourselves. This is done by the manner in which we respond to the people in our lives. The only failure is irresponsible selfishness. Nothing remains to be remembered.

Finally, there is the Pleroma (Greek word): or the **Fulness** or the fulfillment of the person's life. The transition, called death, takes place. Each person enters the full family of mankind to enjoy the person they have become. Everyone will be someone. But some will be wizened, scrawny shrimps because of a totally selfish life. They will be loved for what they are but they are so little.

Heaven is the unending meeting and enjoying of all the people who went before you, lived with you, and came after you. It will be much like the potluck supper with Beilmans and Russells (in Madison, Wisconsin) except you won't have to drive home. Everyone will bring their favorite "dishes". Everyone will circulate and see the interrelation of all people with each other.

How will this happen? I don't know but we keep learning of the interdependence of the genes and the importance of hereditary factors. How could such a plan be stifled without full enjoyment. This would demand eternity. Heavy! But intriguing!

October 19, 1991. Topic: Lois often asked Phil for his perspective.
You asked about people having enemies. The only place on earth where we are certain that human beings get along

perfectly is in the cemetery. Corpses do nothing so they can't bother or challenge anyone. If you are active and accomplishing something, you are sure to irritate someone.

January 19, 1992.

Your Mom enjoyed the get-together. Then as Nyle (brother of Lois) started to play the organ, she got that distant look of deep reverie. She was clearly recalling her past and missing all the people connected with it, especially your Dad. I saw this so often with people as they get older. The familiar faces disappear one by one. Their children and grandchildren were there and enjoyed but part of their life was gone.

I read in the AARP bulletin that many retired persons become alcoholics. Some have had the problem all their lives but as their metabolism slows down the body will not detoxify the alcohol and there is a build-up in the blood. Others begin to drink as their lives slow down, their partners die, their families move away, and they get lonely. These people can be helped to develop new friends and to make sure they do something worthwhile with their time.

February 14, 1993. Topic: Phil enjoyed words and word puzzles.
Happy Valentine's Day! I expressed my feelings and attitudes of the day in the Valentine's card. You have the card so there is no need to repeat. I'll just iterate the same wishes and ideas in this note. "Iterate" is a favorite crossword puzzle entry. I never see it any other place so I want to use it.

May 24, 1993. Topic: Telling stories was part of Phil's fulness of life .
I see the mosquitoes are in the newspaper headlines today. Yet the neighbors were sitting in the grass last evening. I told the neighbors that the Wisconsin mosquitoes had one advantage over the mites here in Iowa. Up in northern Wisconsin, the mosquitoes move the lawn furniture around -- with the people in it. Earl (a neighbor) seemed to doubt my words.

September 12, 1993. Phil enjoyed rides through the country to see places and nature. After the flood waters subsided, Phil & Lois took a drive to follow the Des Moines River to southeast Iowa where it joins the Mississippi River.

We have seen a lot more of Iowa than I had ever thought about. The hegira to the river towns was very interesting.

I really enjoy just driving along and seeing the country itself, then noting all the old and new buildings, the cattle, trees, and crops. I enjoy driving through the old towns. When we talk about the 1850's, I think of my grandparents and their families. When the years reach the 1920's and 30's, they are talking to me of my childhood. Some of the antiques we saw were brand new when I was in grade school (Wichita, Kansas) and Kirkwood (minor seminary in Missouri). Now they look rather primitive. 'Twas a great day!

February 3, 1994.
You asked about contact with people beyond the grave. I think this is one of the principal reasons for the resurrection stories in the Gospels. The writers wanted to point out, first of all, that death is not the end. Each individual lives on as him/herself. There is a difference that was explained because all suffering, pain, and hardships were gone. The person gets around in an entirely different way and the means of communication is different. I think that people who have more intense patterns of feeling or sensation are more apt to have such apparitions (realizations).

May 31, 1994. Topic: Church will not permit women priests.
The anomaly of the situation is absurd. Only women can give birth to a baby - but the men have to baptize them. Women have always prepared most of the meals in the home but they cannot prepare or present the liturgical meal. Mothers have always been the confidants of their children but they can't preside at the Christian Bar Mitzvah which is Confirmation. Mothers have listened to and counseled their children in all problems but only the male ear can listen in confession. The huge majority of those who care for the sick are women but they can't do the ritual for the sick and dying. Marriage is not a marriage unless the woman formally consents.

So what does Holy Orders mean except a fear that someone will show up the emptiness of the vaulted male supremacy?

June 3-6, 1994. Topic: 25th wedding anniversary
The weekend in Wisconsin was a grand celebration. It was delightful riding to and from Madison - cloudburst and all.

Several times I caught myself comparing Jacqui with the little girl we first meet and adopted years ago. She has weathered many a personal bout and has become a pleasant, forthright, efficient person. Ron has grown into a great young man.

Now it's onward to the next phase. I see my work as writing up and filling in the picture I gave to people years ago in Bible classes and study clubs.

January 26, 1995.

I'll bring up the death of Wayne although I don't have a lot to say (brother of Lois who died with no warning 1 week after a family celebration, died of complications of a viral infection). I've known Wayne since 1967 when we first went to visit your folks when I was giving a retreat to nuns in Carroll.

Now I see Wayne's death in a positive light. Your Dad enjoyed Wayne immensely and now they are together to visit about all the years. Wayne will still have strong interest in the details on earth but he'll stir the courts of heaven as he cruises around.

Additional information: Wayne had a wide variety of friends and always did enjoy "cruising", driving around, with them. His wife, 3 married daughters, grandchildren, and all of us miss him.

February 4, 1995.

A combination of one of my "Word to the Wise" (Phil's) newspaper columns, our trip to Oklahoma where you lead the workshop, and Wayne's death stirred up a night of intriguing thoughts for me. The newspaper topic was about spring. The idea was that if we looked at the field in January and February, we could never believe anything would live again. Yet as we saw on the trip, some of the fields in Oklahoma and Kansas were already starting to green up for the spring. This made me think of planting potatoes.

We used to cut the potatoes and then plant them. Later the new plant came up, bloomed, and in June (in Kansas) we started digging new potatoes. Very often the little piece of planted potato would be clinging to the roots, all dried up. But there would be 8 or 10 nice new potatoes.

Jesus used this very example for the meaning of death. If the seed doesn't die, it remains alone. If it dies, it brings forth a whole new crop. So death is the stepping stone to new life. What is it like? Christ risen gives some answers. Mary Magdalene looked right at him and didn't recognize him until he spoke. Then he would suddenly appear and disappear.

Theologians spoiled all of these ideas with "divinity". Christ was a super talented & gifted kid. He figured out how the whole wisdom of his ancestors should be interpreted. He taught all this and said the proof or goal is bringing this world to "completion".

How do we do it? He emphasized that it had to be by "Koinonia" - the Greek word for "sharing". Once we really establish human sharing, we'll stop stupid and useless wars, fights, and destruction. Cooperation will bring total completion. When a person dies, the only questions asked are "Who did you become?" "How did you further human growth and harmony?"

We are "becoming" by our teaching, writing, and contacts with people. We're on the way. Your brother Wayne is now in heaven, or whatever you call the new home. He is learning, enjoying, and waiting for us.

February 13-14, 1995.

The Latin phrase *"Requiescat in Pace",* which is usually translated as "Rest in Peace", would be a final wish that would be translated "Enjoy yourself totally and worry about nothing." We need some more realistic description of "eternal" and "peace". The first Christians had them; "churches" lost them.

April 8, 1995.

I thought a lot about the topic of burial since last night. The whole bit of embalming and burial of the corpse is an American custom. When the GI's were in Italy, they saw that a person was cleaned up and buried a few hours after death. Then the next day or a couple days later there was a funeral Mass with the catafalque. Two of these clever Americans went to Italy and opened a mortuary and offered to embalm. They starved until they took different jobs to get money to come home to U.S. The Europeans saw no need of embalming.

What body do we get at the Resurrection? Magdalene did not recognize Jesus until he spoke. People will still be the same person but the body will be in good shape at some ideal age.

I'm going to make or type and sign a statement that I want to be cremated. Then you or someone can scatter the dust where you will. LaBelle* sounds fine or any body of water near at hand. If I outlast you, I'll scatter the dust where you want. The dust is not you. You are the person that continues on without problems or headaches.

* Additional information: Lake LaBelle is at Oconomowoc, Wisconsin, the location of major seminary. After he was ordained a priest, he taught at the seminary. So Lake LaBelle, and the many lakes in the area, held many good memories for Phil. Some memorial will be placed near this area.

July 12-13, 1995.
I mulled over several of the Biblical topics in my head yesterday. I have a lot more work to do on the notion of heaven or life after this life. I think there is more to be developed if I get into the right Biblical passages.

August 13, 1995.
You asked what I (Phil) would do if you (Lois) died first. First of all, I would expect a few visits from you from the next world. I'm sure you could shake somebody loose in that department - Peter, Thomas Aquinas, Augustine. Let Paul alone. You would just start a fight with him over some of his ideas. You would get along with Luke and John very well. Of the ladies, I'm sure the mother of Jesus would be smiling and telling you a lot of your requests for information and procedures would have to go higher up. I have no doubt you would be at the center with Yahweh himself, questioning some of his decisions on the making and running of the universe. Given the equivalent of about 2 years, you would have charge of some of the programs and be organizing some workshops or field trips.

As for me, I would play it by ear. I envision some work with Bible writing - somehow.

October 25, 1995.
You mentioned the resurrection last night. This was a question thrown at Paul in his missionary groups. The people had not seen Christ and they questioned Paul's sanity. His answer was clear: "If Christ did not rise from the dead in reality, we are of all fools the greatest." As Paul saw it, the teachings of

40

Jesus were fine but the evidence for the truth and value of these teachings depended on the resurrection from the dead. Jesus stressed that his resurrection was the prototype of all that came after him.

The body will be the same so that it is immediately recognized. I see it in the sprouting of every seed. The tulip bulb, for example, doesn't look like much. Yet the bulb sprouts and the plant comes forth and there is the beautiful flower. No one could imagine or predict it. The same is true of the human body. The resurrection will be the full flowering. Just as planting the seed is essential to getting the harvest, so death is the course to full life.

I'm not trying to convince you of physical resurrection. You'll rise from the dead when the time comes. In the meantime, my love and support are all yours.

December 2, 1995.

I'm sorry to hear about the death of your Uncle Clarence. He is now with his wife and relatives and friends, and reliving past glories and making new experiences. His family will miss him.

December 13, 1995.

Circumstances: It's about 2 weeks before Bill , brother of Lois, dies of cancer. This will be her second brother to die in 1995.

There is no doubt that your brother, Bill, has received his final notice. Marita (his wife) and he and the family have accepted this fully. Bill already has his eyes turned on the next stage of his life. Those he leaves behind will miss him but remember he is going to join your Dad and Wayne and the rest of the family. Heaven is not a new life. It is the fulness of this life. And as Christ pointed out, there is no way this can be described until we get there.

Everyone gets into heaven but how fully each person can participate will depend on how fully that person prepared in this life. The actions of this life build the capacity to receive and act in the next life. Christ says explicitly that the criterion is how much of your life was a life of **service** to others. The selfish person will be the "runt".

December 20, 1995.

We talked about a lot of questions last night. I'll write my answer to them a day at a time. Today, I'll take the notion of death in what I see as the real Christian sense.

As the Old Testament ended, there was serious question as to what lay beyond death. The Jews had settled it for themselves in the early post-exilic writings, about 500 B.C. For the Jews who lived and died faithful to the prescriptions of the Torah, they were welcomed into the bosom of Abraham. The unfaithful were excluded from Abraham's presence. The place of exclusion was a constantly burning fire in the Valley of Hinnon or Gehenna. There was no interaction between the two groups.

In the New Testament, all those who lived by the law of "love" went to the presence of God the Father and the whole family of man. Jesus spells out explicitly what is the basis for inclusion in the sentence: Everything depended on how your life was lived in the **service** of your family, friends, neighbors, people you worked with and for, and strangers. The demands were not gigantic: You were to share what you have and what you are. If you shared, you were identified as a child of the Father. If you did not share, you excluded yourself from the family. Hence only selfish, egotistical, self-righteous persons will be excluded.

December 21, 23-24. 1995.

Comments on funeral of Bill, brother of Lois, who died from cancer - diagnosed in Sept. and after aggressive chemo therapy, died in Dec.

Marita (Bill's wife) talked a lot about Bill when she sat down in his chair. The main drift of everything she said was that they had ample preparation. They had discussed practically every issue that could come up. She could honestly say she knew exactly what he thought.

The loss of Bill was a cause of sorrow but I must say it turns my attention more and more to the meaning and happiness of the "new" life. It will be the next step in living but it will be as different as the life of a tiny baby compared with the full life of an adult.

January 1, 1996.

I look back to see the successes and to enjoy them again. The sad events over which I have no control, I put out of mind because mulling them over does no good and changes nothing.

Death is one of those events. Death is an event toward which we are all headed. It is not a sad event for the person who dies if he/she has lived a life of sharing, working and growing. The person who dies comes into true fulfillment and enjoys all who have gone before.

For the people left behind, there is a sad parting but there is the surety of meeting again. Death is not unfair. It is just a question of when the body wears out. For some people this can be over 90 years. For others it can be much less.

I know this is a detached way of viewing a significant departure but it is the most fruitful way for me.

March 29, 1996.

I think that people who die after living a good life such as your brothers Bill and Wayne and your Dad get their new bodies immediately. They aren't floating around like some invisible blob. They are just like Jesus was between his resurrection and ascension. They mingle freely with each other and are aware of what is happening with those left behind. Once in a while they can contact people here on earth but most of the time they have to let us work out our own lives.

They are not gone. We just can't see them but they are enjoying each other in a very real world called Eden. When we finish our lives, we'll go to meet them.

Christian life is not a structured pattern imposed on our regular life. Christian life is our day-to-day existence lived in sharing with each other. It may be our neighbor picking up the mail for us when we are gone, you buying me a new shirt you think I'd like or need, a teacher patting a little child on the shoulder. It is the service of every day existence.

Our whole lives as teachers have been lives of service and giving. We have no idea what influence we have had. A few people come back to tell us. Most keep on living.

Heaven is just perfect sharing with those who know and love you, and always meeting new people.

May 1, 1996.

The night we took your mom for a ride around Black Hawk Lake, she came alive in a special way as she pointed out where she and your dad used to fish. Death will not be an end for her but a reunion and a full life. This is the basic teaching of the Christian faith for centuries. There are some efforts to hold people by "fear" tactics of hellfire and damnation but those tactics are unchristian. The only source of exclusion from full life in heaven is a failure to be kind to people. This is the only criterion laid down in the gospels. The actual judgment scene in Matthew states the sentence in these very words.

May 19, 1996. Situation: Phil's sister, Mary, was dying.

Denny, Mary's son, spoke to me about his conviction that people who are dying are already in contact with those in the next world. He was real happy to hear I agreed completely and added to his ideas.

May 29, 1996.

Roland Murphy (Biblical Scholar - like Phil) said that the phrase "Rest in Peace" is really a pagan Roman phrase. I didn't argue with him (over the phone) but I've heard this before and I know it is not true.

The Romans talked constantly about "Pax". The Roman peace was definitely a cessation of war. They greeted each other with the "Pax embrace" and always sent people on their way with the phrase "Vode in Pace." Christ and his apostles certainly knew this.

So in John's account of the Last Supper, Jesus says explicitly, "My peace I give you- not as the world gives peace." (not Roman pax). Then Christ describes what his peace is.

The Christians used the Roman greeting with the Christian meaning. Gradually, the liturgy fell back to the pagan notion.

Talking to Roland Murphy, yesterday, kicked off a lot of memories. He sounded totally surprised that I continue to use the background in Sacred Scripture that I have. According to him, most of the men that left the active priesthood, did not use their educational background.

There is also no doubt I used it to the full teaching at Upper Iowa University, in my writings, and as background for teaching social studies. The twice-weekly newspaper column, "Word to the Wise" (1982-1994) reached a lot of people. The commentary on the Bible (I'm currently writing) will do much more.

After talking with Roland, I'm more satisfied and happy that I am out of that closed circle.

June 11, 1996.

The more I hear of people seeing dead relatives, the more I understand and accept it. This was commonly accepted teaching until 1st Vatican Council (1869-1870) and the morose aspect of afterlife that was imposed on the theology and popular preaching. It was much easier to scare the people and get Mass stipends than to motivate them and give them hope and encouragement.

June 12, 1996. Mary Clark, sister of Philip, dies. Ed, Mary's husband, and
their children will surely miss her cheerful and dedicated care.
I'm sure my sister Mary made a real stir in heaven as soon as she entered. I like that idea of God as a kindly loving Father gathering all his family to him and getting them all acquainted with each other, sharing all their good times, and finding family ties all the way back (an idea expressed in Mary's eulogy). It would take an eternity just to do that.

July 18, 1996.

The judgment scene at the end of Matthew's Gospel is the best picture of the whole idea. "Come, blessed of my father! Enter into the kingship (or be kinged) as intended from the beginning. For I was hungry, and you fed me, etc." The judgment scene is exactly like the checker game. Death is the moment when a person reaches the other end of the board. Then he/she is "kinged" and can enjoy total happiness forever. Each move on the board was an action of daily life.

July 27, 1996. Application: What is expected of us after our beloved in departed?
The "Spirit" couldn't come until Jesus left. This was really true. The first followers would be totally dependent on him as long as

he was around. When he left, they would be able to get moving on their own.

July 30, 1996. (Phil's comments on doctor-assisted suicide)

There is no reason why a person should suffer uselessly in a terminal state. Pain and suffering have no value in themselves and doctors have worked to remove it all times. Jesus escaped from his suffering and death on several occasions. Finally, he decided there was no escape, so he let himself be taken.

I see no reason why a person cannot consciously ask for help to die. This decision cannot be foisted on them but it is theirs to make.

August 1, 1996.

You asked why I was pensive last night. I deliberately did not say because I would have become worse. I read the article on good and evil in THE NEW YORKER magazine and really appreciated it. But the aftermath was a real irritation with popes, bishops and theologians through the centuries as they "created" more and more sins.

The last two years in Oconomowoc (major seminary) we spent 6.5 hours a week in "moral" theology and 4 hours a week in Canon (church) Law. All that time was spent on "sins" and the ways in which the human being is immoral and bad. Then the CSsR's (Redemptorists - religious order to which Phil belonged) parish missions and retreats were 95% talk about hell, sin, damnation and fear. I did not buy it and I changed my approach as soon as I started to work with people. All these thoughts and feelings were roiling around in my head. Finally, I got it under control.

The same is true of the picture of Jesus. I am thoroughly convinced that novice master, Father John Zellar, had arrived at understanding the complete humanity of Jesus in the early 1930's. His presentation of Christ was so real in the Novitiate. However, he could not say a lot of this publicly.

Jesus was a gifted young man who saw clearly where the world should be headed. He and his cousin talked about these ideas for years. Then both of them, Jesus and John the Baptist, felt the inner drive to do something about it. Luke's gospel stresses that Christ was always afraid of the end result.

September 2, 1996.
I like what the New Testament gospels tell us about this after-life. After Jesus was raised from the dead, he was the same person. He had the same body, even to the points of scars and eating. Yet he was totally different and was going to full union with those who had gone before.

March 5, 1997.
As I listen to your objection to the plan as narrated in Old Testament, I am sitting next to Job about the 3rd century BC. He was a man who had gone far beyond any commandments or laws to be kind, generous and holy. And he was "shit on" literally. A bird did it to Tobit but everything conspired against Job. Finally Job cried out for an answer.

His answer was "You'll have to understand and see the whole plan first." That we cannot do until we enter into our final phase through death. We say the same thing to kids in the field of education constantly. When a bright student starts probing, we encourage them to dig and we see their frustration at not getting the whole picture or all the answers at once.

March 26, 1997.
I don't see how the dire picture of heaven, hell or purgatory ever got such a strong hold. Even in the worst translation of the Bible and early writings, it is impossible. The Old Testament presents only the "Bosom of Abraham". If you did not live up to the Law sincerely, you were banished to Sheol - the place of no identity. In the New Testament, it is the contrast between the presence of the Father (identity) and the Valley of Hinnom (no identity). The criterion was/is: *How did you treat your fellow human beings?*

May 19, 1997.
You brought up communications between people in this world or life and the next stage of life. I definitely think there are interplays if the person on this side is receptive and capable of receiving. As I've told you so often, your sensitivity to the future is extraordinary. I have no doubt you can and do communicate with your Dad and brothers, Bill and Wayne.

There have been many instances of such communications in the past but usually some churchman got hold of the person and used him/her for his own purposes or stifled the person.

November 24, 1997. Occasion: Phil's birthday 11/23. Phil & Lois brought
   the food and had the birthday dinner at Norma and Fred Kennebeck's
   house because Lois's Mom was at Norma's. Norma is a sister
   to Lois and Fred is Norma's husband.

Thank you very much for a fine birthday celebration. Everyone enjoyed the banquet. Fred said we could have that type of party at their house any time we wanted. If we didn't have an occasion, he would think of one for us.

November 26, 1997.

Norma just called with the news about Fred. She found him dead in bed this morning. Fred has now entered the next and final stage of his life.

I (Phil) told Norma that Fred had spoken to me at length about dying the other night when I was sitting in the kitchen with him. He was certainly ready to go.

November 27, 1997.

We miss people who are gone before us but they can still keep in contact if they are needed or see fit.

January 17, 1998.

We don't have time to look into the past in a negative fashion. Some plans went awry but that's the nature of human actions. Some plans work according to schedule and some don't. So we have to look at what we have and move forward.

April 8, 1998.

I marvel at the way my Dad kept trying in spite of one bad year after another. The good years were 1912-29. Edward (Phil's brother) was killed in an accident in '29; '30 was a dry year; then the depression. In spite of all, Pop never crumbled as many did.

June 24, 1998.

Yesterday, as I was reading Edersheim's LIFE OF CHRIST, I was more and more impressed by the simplicity of the teaching of Jesus. He often stressed one point: The Christian way of life is sharing with others in every need. The whole judgment at the end of life is based on this one point.

November 1-2, 1998. Topic: Discussing All Saints' Day and All Souls' Day.
When you die, God is not sitting there as some stern judge. Christ's picture was very simple. Answer the one question, *"How did you respond to the needs of the people around you?"* This "sharing" or "harmony" determines how much you could enjoy all of eternity. This point is crystal clear in the Gospels according to Luke, Matthew and John. The Letter of James makes one statement about prayer for the dead and on that, theologians and popes built a whole theology of guilt and punishment.

December 25, 1998.
Situation: Phil & Lois stayed with Lois's Mom Christmas eve so her sister and husband, Jean Marie and Lenus Thelen, could accept a dinner invitation. Christmas eve ritual is: Phil read Nativity story from Bible, Christmas songs are sung, gifts are opened. The Roets' drove back to Des Moines after Jean Marie and Lenus returned - about 110 miles trip.

We certainly had a busy and pleasant Christmas eve. We read Luke's Christmas story; sang carols; visited with your Mom, Nyle and Mary, Jean and Lenus; and had a very easy drive home on an "All is calm; all is bright" night. At home, the hot water of the shower felt like heaven.

February 4, 1999.
Topic: importance of studying Bible in original languages to understand its original meaning and then see how it applies to today's living.
Two of the most important Biblical words are "Bara" (Aramaic) to "beget at a son" and "to telos" (Greek). "To telos" means "end" in the sense of "complete fulness". So when we talk of the end of the world we are not speaking about a moment when the whole world disintegrates. Rather, we are talking about the world when it is brought to its completion or fulfillment.

We need only think of all the progress that has been made in the last fifty years by way of discoveries and inventions and we can see that the "telos" is an ongoing process.

When Jesus was dying on the cross, his last word was

"tetelestai". He bowed his head and died. This is the verbal form of "telos" and means "I have accomplished all I set out to do".

August 27-29, 1999.
The first stage of this "fulfillment" was Christ on the Cross and his word "tetelestai" meaning "It is complete!" He had established the pattern by which the plan can be followed and completed - harmony and sharing. Now it's up to us.

October 15-18, 19, 20, 1999. "to telos" - "completion, perfection, fulness".
I have the Biblical monograph on "to telos" well along and know exactly where I want it to go. Now I have to bring all the ideas together. The more I work on the ideas, the more I am convinced the world will not be destroyed but "brought to perfection, completion" to be enjoyed by all who identify themselves. (Oct 15-18)

Last night and this morning, I really did a lot of thinking about the "final perfection" (telos) of the whole universe. The Biblical picture is very clear. God started everything off with all of the potency for development. As is stated, God saw that it was good and he was very pleased. Then he turned it over to mankind to develop all the potentialities in the whole universe. When it is truly complete it will have people with firm conviction, true sharing with each other, sharing in powers of real kingship, and a love that is true harmony. We have a way to go! (Oct 19)

I have finally reduced the whole Bible story to two phrases: "From 'Bara' to 'To Telos' ". The story begins in the "Fatherhood of God" and will be complete in the "Brotherhood of Man." . Oct 20)

Additional Information from editor:
"Bara" is the second word in Genesis. It means to "beget as a son". "To telos" is defined above. The whole picture is:
The Brotherhood of Man because of the Fatherhood of God.

December 29-30, 1999.
Your Aunt Lizzie certainly looked at peace (in coffin). As I looked as her, I could easily visualize her with her husband and other members of the family in heaven. She would be able to meet and chat with the students she had taught years ago. Theology has made such a hassle out of the "beatific vision" and

other things of the after life.

Jesus describes it perfectly in Matthew. "Come family members! Enter into the joy of your Dad (Father). You shared with others so now we can enjoy each other." It's a big family get-together that never ends. All share together what happened here on earth and then go on to share new things, each day. There are always new people to meet. Before, we just read or heard about them.

The way of life that Jesus taught and lived is simple and solid. It's the fulfillment of the plan intended by Yahweh from the beginning. It is so well stated in the opening chapter of Genesis. The world is here for us to discover and use together.

As I read and heard about the recent trip to the moon and the work of the astronauts mending the broken part, I could just see God smiling and waving his hand in approval. We are just beginning to unlock all the good things he planted here. And he said it was our job to discover and use them.

January 10, 2000.
Circumstances: Phil will go for angiogram this morning and remain in the
    hospital for 4 bypasses. My back had gone into spasm as it often does
    under stress. And Phil, instead of asking help from Jesus on his behalf,
    is talking to Jesus on my behalf - another example of Phil's generous love.
        This is an excerpt from his note before we went to the hospital.

After I finished reading to you last night (Phil read to Lois to help her fall asleep), I talked to Jesus Christ in very clear terms. I reminded him of all the people he had helped and healed. I urged him to do away with your pain and give you a good night's sleep.

Since I have written so much about Jesus in my commentaries on the Gospels, I feel I have a much better acquaintance with him. I am sure he is aware of us just as truly as the members of our families are.

I can see the people of your family and mine mixing with each other, and see Jesus making sure he gets around to all of them. I also have special words for Peter, John, Philip, Luke and Matthew. They are ordinary men who did well and received their new status. (Phil joined them 10/29/02)

March 22-24, 2000, and April 1-2, 2000.
Topic: Phil enjoyed observing nature, wildlife, prairies, waters, and seasons.

The visit to the Neal Smith Prairie Learning Center was very delightful, yesterday. The video about the prairie brought a lot of memories back. I walked behind a plow and a team of horses when I was 8 years old, 1929, on the Oliver place (farm where Roets family lived.) My Dad would plow the first round on each field. Then I took over. He would make that first furrow straight. Then I just had to follow in his lead. Sometimes the work was a bit tough when we were turning a prairie hay field into truck garden.

I think we have doves making a nest in the fir tree in the backyard. Two doves have been flying in and out while I am sitting here writing this note. They should feel very safe in that tree and its location.

May 27-29, 2000. Situation: Lois's mom, Mary Schelle, dies at age 97.

My sympathy is with you for the death of your mother. It's hard to lose someone to whom you have strong attachment for over 60 years. However, there is a brighter side to the picture for your Mom. She has shed the worn-out, pain-ridden body and gone to be with your Dad, your two brothers, and all the members of your family and her family that have gone before her. They can share all the happiness that is their due.

Mary will help your brother, Nyle, adjust as he was hit hard by your Mom's death. (Mary is Nyle's wife).

Matthew (gospel) calls death the entering into the fulness of the "kingship" as described by Jesus here on earth. Luke says it is the fulness of "koinonia" (Greek word for "sharing") with each other. John says that now people can enjoy the fulness of true love.

We can look back and recall all the good times you shared with your Dad and Mom and family. Your mother had a very calm, peaceful transition from this life to the next.

May 30-June 3, 2000.

Your Mom looked beautiful as she was prepared for burial. However, that was no longer your Mom. It was the body in which she had lived and worked, bore her family, and cared for them. Your mother is the person who dwelt in that body for 97 years. At the end of time, she gets a new body which will be totally beautiful and without flaw.

I met your folks the first time in 1967, when I was still active as a priest. (Phil was giving a retreat to the nuns in Carroll, Iowa, about 12 miles from Lois's parents: Charles and Mary Schelle). Then I knew her for 31 years since we are married. As you have said so often she was always a "doer". She prepared meals, quilted, visited easily, spoke her mind, and was always grateful and gracious for anything done for her.

As you continue your life, concentrate on all the good times you had with your Dad and Mom. We took them on trips that they appreciated very much. There were times when you were separated from them. That is a part of living. So I would stress recalling and talking about all the good times you have had.

Then, when we die, we go to meet all that are gone before us. As Matthew says, "I was hungry and you fed me. I needed clothes and a home and you took care of my needs. I was sick and you cared for me." That is the recipe for complete happiness. John says simply "Life and love are service."

June 26-27, 2000.
In the Christian ideal of resurrection, each of us is going to rise a full person when the world is complete. We will be the person we made during our life in this world. Jesus could easily have been raised from the dead, the fully developed person he became, in order to encourage his followers.

June 29-30, 2000.
The secret to the Kingdom of God established by Christ is spelled out explicitly in Matthew 28 at the judgment scene in each person's life. Entrance into the eternal kingdom depends entirely on how people reacted to each other in this life. If they were truly aware of the needs of others and responded to them, they establish their eternal home. If this sharing was not present, there is no place for them. In this life, there will be difficulty, hardship -- but there is happiness promised if the attitude is right.

September 9-11, 2000.
There have been many theories or beliefs about death and the hereafter by different people and cultures. I like what we

are given in the Bible - Old and New Testament. According to the Genesis picture, there would have been no death before Adam's failure. Then the Jews came up with going to be with Abraham. Then Jesus comes along with the entrance into the eternal kingdom of the Father - the Family or Brotherhood of Mankind entering into the Fatherhood of God.

We are recognized as the person we were -- as was Jesus when he was seen after the resurrection. The marks of the wounds were still there. Yet we will be totally different, as was Jesus the same day for Mary Magdalene and the two disciples on the road to Emmaus.

October 27, 2000.

You asked what heaven is like according to the Biblical notion. In the Old Testament, the afterlife - if it was good - was to be in the "lap of Abraham". This meant that all the Jews who had lived lives according to the Torah would be happy and live with all other faithful Jews. The unfaithful would be tossed into Sheol which was a place of total loneliness and frustration.

In the New Testament, Christ very clearly tells us what the life after death really is. It was not something mysterious but fulfilling.

In Matthew's picture it is the full and total **sharing** with everyone. All the different aspects of this sharing are explained in all the qualities of the kingship as Matthew develops it.

John has identically the same notion except he calls it **service**. "Anyone who says he loves God whom he cannot see, and does not love his neighbor whom he can see, is a liar and the truth is not in him." Heaven will be a place of perfect love.

So right now, the members of your family and mine who have departed are enjoying each other.

July 20-25, 2001. Situation: trip to Wichita, Kansas, to attend funeral of Phil's younger brother, Francis.

I was glad we were able to go to Wichita for the funeral of Francis. After Martha died, (wife of Francis who died 10 years before him) Francis's joy of life left him. He was like an empty shell. He got diabetes and that added further problems.

I met people at the funeral I had not seen for years - some since 1948 when I was ordained a priest. My generation in both Roets and Lohkamp families are almost all passed on.

Francis and Martha are together again and happy.

October 7-16, 2001.

As I looked at the beautiful fall trees on the way to the post office and the bank, I thought of what the changing of the leaves means. In the spring, the leaves "bud out" and we are all happy that spring has returned. Then for a whole summer, these leaves fill the air with the elements we need for breathing. They form a chain with the roots of the tree to keep its life-cycle rolling. Then in the fall, the leaves give up the green and adopt all the gorgeous colors, to announce the fruits of the fall and the preparation for winter.

These brilliant colors are shown to remind us that the leaves did not die. They completed their work and now will collect for their next stage in the cycle of nature.

January 21, 2002.

Jesus had grown up in the midst of a "hate-full" world. He saw it all around him. He saw the response of Rome and the Caesars to this world. They would stop the hate by physical force and set up a different kind of military supremacy where most of the world were abject slaves.

Out of this milieu, Jesus saw the only solution: Sincere respect and love had to take over and the human dignity of every person had to be upheld. He convinced a handful of people and they continued his work.

June 18, 2002.

Authority is to be the leadership of the Shepherd (pastor) and the firmness of the Kepha (foundation stone). As a pastor, authority is to be out in front leading and calling all to follow to the green pasture, fresh water, afternoon rest, and the safety of the fold at night. As the Kepha, authority is to be the firm foundation on which all confidence is based. The shepherd figure stresses how well the leaders must know the personalities and needs of the flock and how to minister to each. The Kepha stresses that firmness of the sharing or community is found in the leader. Peter was called "Kepha" when Jesus selected him as leader.

The picture is simple.

Sweetheart,

Good evening. I just closed the curtains. It's starting to go to the dark side of the day. I ate the chicken and carrots. The carrots were excellent and the chicken was good.

My brother, Tom, called from Florida this afternoon. Celie (Cecilia, Phil's older sister) had called him and told him I was going in for surgery. He was an RN in the Marines for 20 years. He is worried about the war in the Middle East. One of his boys is in the Marines and the other is in the Army. Both are already in the Middle East.

Thanks for all you have done and are doing for me. I really appreciate your concern and all the details you have taken care of. I certainly would have avoided this whole "mess" (cancer of the bladder and the bladder will be surgically removed) but I have nothing to say about that. While I was sitting in my chair this morning, I looked at the picture of the Good Shepherd and suggested that he use some of his power to clear up my medical problems. He just smiled and said nothing.

I watched the News and Bush's face (George W) was on several times as he was trying to explain his position (to go to war). He was getting a cold reception.

We have some rain in the forecast for the next days but not much other news.

I love you, Sweetie, ex imo corde, Phil

Lois added these entries to Volume 92 (Phil's last journal):

10-20-02.

At 2:30 a.m, on 9/25/02, Phil was taken to the hospital as there was bleeding with clots of blood spurting from around the catheter (placed there after Sept 16th surgery). The drainage could not be cleared (in emergency room) and Phil was admitted to the hospital. He hasn't been home since.

The surgery the 26th was successful (removal of cancerous bladder) but many problems developed.

10-30-02.

Phil died last night at 5:45 p.m. I was with him, holding his hand, reviewing our favorite memories, recalling names of students he taught and places we lived, reciting passages from the Bible, reading from his writings, and singing short passages of favorite songs or melodies. I held him and his hand. He gave two deliberate squeezes of my hand as a final farewell - the same type of hand-squeeze we often did in life when one of us needed reassurance or courage or strength. I assured him that he was much loved. He was the joy of my life, and the source of strength and courage for me and many others.

Phil's breath became more shallow and then the breath and heart quietly and peacefully stopped. The words I can remember saying when there was no breath for quite awhile were: *"Come, blessed of my Father. Enter into the kingdom of heaven prepared for you. Join your Mother and Father. I will always love you and miss you."*

Our 33.5 years of marriage and 36 years of friendship in this life were over. I shall miss him.

Philip G. Roets Lives

Philip G. Roets lives in many of us. Many more will know of his legacy through publications - written and audio - and through memories you share with others. It's important that his examples of fulness of life, and the knowledge and value of the Bible live on.

Appreciation to Family, Friends, Colleagues and Students in Phil's Classes.

Many thanks to you who were Phil's friends, colleagues and students during his almost 81 years of life. Some of you are mentioned in this book; more are mentioned in Phil's complete journals. Many more lived in him and in his memories and values. Phil gave love and trust cautiously for fear they would be rejected as unwanted gifts. He gave and valued loyalty and friendship.

Family was important to Phil. Special **thanks** to Phil's sister Cecilia and her daughter, Charlotte, who came to the hospital while Phil could still visit, and returned for the funeral visitation. They were also our hosts when we visited Wichita. Jacqueline (daughter) arrived from New Jersey while Phil could still recognize her and appreciate her words of support, love, and gratitude. Many of Lois's family came to visit us at home, at the hospital, and funeral visitation. Support and love from family and friends were and are appreciated. *Let's continue it.*

Information on Phil's Journals/Notes to Lois

Philip Roets wrote notes/journals to his wife, Lois, from June 9, 1979, their 10th wedding anniversary, until September 24, 2002, the evening before entering the hospital. Phil never returned home alive. Topics in the journals were many: personal thoughts, history, politics, incidents and people related to teaching or places we lived, religion - especially Catholics and the Bible, nature and weather, thoughts on special events, encouragement and support of each other and our work, and expression of love for each other.

An example of a journal entry in Phil's own handwriting is on the next page. It is part of entry dated 6/19/02.

There is no place in the N. T. that speaks of belonging to a "church". Jesus always talks of living in the society in which you are and bringing alive his ideas and ideals. Paul was the only one who founded separate groups much as the Jews had done. Only toward the end of his letters did he begin to get the full notion that Christ talked about. I think that was due to St. Luke. He edited all the letters in keeping with his picture as developed in the Gospel according to Luke.

The Church drifted farther and farther into the quagmire of rules and laws & rubrics. The fight with Luther & the Council of Trent sounded the death knell. On the TV program, the other night, the speaker said the first light was seen in John XXIII. Then he died and the old ideas revived.

I love you, Sweetie! Eximo corda!
Phil

59

Lifeline for Philip G. Roets STL, SSL

11/13/21 -- Born in Wichita, Kansas, to Philip and Pauline (Lohkamp) Roets. He loved and admired his parents, and 15 brothers and sisters.

1927-1935 - Elementary Education: St. Joseph's School. Wichita.

1935-1941.- Minor Seminary. St. Joseph's Seminary and College, Kirkwood, Missouri. 4 years high school and 2 college.

1941-1942.- Novitiate: religious order of Redemptorists (CSsR).

1942-1948.- Major Seminary. Oconomowoc, Wisconsin.
Two years philosophy and 4 years theology.
Tutored fellow students in Latin and other subjects.
Coordinated the "snow removal" crew; raised rabbits.

June 6, 1948.- Ordained Catholic priest.

1948, summer. - First assignment as priest was to St. Louis where he helped take parish census and began work with the deaf - a lifelong interest and service.

1948-1951.- Catholic University in Washington D.C. Earned Licentiate in Theology, STL, plus Semitic languages. He worked on translating the Dead Sea Scrolls. While in D.C. he did much parish work on weekends in DC, NJ, VA, and NY. He also assisted the military chaplain at Fort Meyer, VA, with religious services and education classes.

1951-1952.- Pontifical Biblical Institute, Rome, Italy.
Completed the Licentiate in Sacred Scripture, SSL.
Exams from May 12 to June 8, 1952, included:
33 hrs-written, 11 hrs-orals, and 1 hour defense of thesis.
Phil's best memories of Rome include seeing great art, learning from outstanding teachers and fellow students from around the world, and seeing historic places. He also added Italian to his list of languages.

1948-1969.- Career as Catholic Priest:
Taught at Redemptorists Seminary, Oconomowoc, WI
Taught Ethics for School of Nursing,
St. Mary's Hospital, Madison, WI
Retreats for high school students in Minneapolis
and adults at Retreat House, Oconomowoc.

Numerous retreats and Days of Recollection in
WI, IA, MN, MI, KS, OK, east coast.
Series of lectures on Bible for clergy and educators in
Wisconsin, Iowa, east coast, Kentucky.
Visiting counselor/chaplain for Vets Hospital in
Waukesha, WI, and Fort Meyer. VA.
Guided Bible Study Clubs in family neighborhoods.
Advisor and confessor to religious men & women
in Wisconsin - on a weekly basis.
Advisor and counselor to many who sought his help.
Teacher/lecturer on Old and New Testament
studies on weekends and summer (in addition
to regular teaching at the seminary and
conducting retreats). Audio tapes of some
of these lectures still exist.
St. Norbert's College. DePere, WI
Viterbo University, LaCrosse, WI
Alverno College, Milwaukee, WI
Seminarians, priests, nuns in WI, IA.

June 7, 1969.-Married Lois Schelle at Catholic Church in Rio, WI.

1969-1980. Taught 6th grade in Pardeeville, WI, and enjoyed it.
Began writing Commentaries on the Bible and
Wildlife Series for students.
Wrote first draft of <u>Books of the Bible.</u>

1980. Presented paper "The Spirit of Yahweh: A study of the
meaning of the word 'Spirit' in the Bible." at the
annual meeting of the Catholic Biblical Association
(CBA) at Duluth, MN.

October, 1980 - Move to Iowa for family-related reasons.

1980-1981.- Taught science to 8th graders. Oskaloosa, Iowa.
(Long-long substitute for the year). Phil had natural
talent and life-long interest in science - all areas.

1981- 1988.-Taught remedial reading and math for grades 3-8;
taught acceleration and enrichment in
reading for kindergarteners. New Sharon, IA..
Taught graduate courses to teachers "Reading
Strategies I" and "Reading Strategies II".
Wrote booklet "200 Considerations to Promote
Mental Health" and did workshops on it.

Continued studying and translating Old and New
Testament from original languages.
Continued commentaries on OT & NT.
Translated Biblical quotations for each day of the
year. Wrote rote booklet "200 Encouraging
Quotes and Notes from the Bible."

1982-1994. Wrote a twice-weekly newspaper column "Word to
the Wise" for the Oskaloosa Herald. Oskaloosa, IA.

1988 - fall. Phil and Lois move to Des Moines, Iowa.

1989-1994. Phil taught on Des Moines campus for Upper Iowa
University: Spanish I, Spanish II, Business
Ethics, Intro to Philosophy, and Philosophy of
Religion. This last course used Phil's book
Books of the Bible (1992) as textbook.
Tutored elementary and high school students in
reading, French, Italian, composition.
Continued writing commentaries on Bible.
Began monographs on Biblical themes.

June, 1994.-Celebrated 25th wedding anniversary in IA, WI.
Retired from formal teaching and tutoring.

1995-2002. Continued writing commentaries on Bible and Biblical
themes. Some themes were not complete at the time
of his death but 1000+ pages were completed.

1982-2002. Accompanied and assisted his wife, Lois, on
her workshops on education of the gifted.

1969-2002 Enjoyed family, friends, and neighborhood events.

1948-2002. Taught sign language and was "on call" in
communities to assist the deaf.
Gave counsel and spiritual guidance on individual
basis to those who requested help.

1960's - 2002. Publications:
Audio tapes of lectures on Bible.
Translation from French. The New Testament,
Always New. by author Charpentier.
200 Considerations to Promote Mental Health,
A Pocket Companion to Wisdom,
Books of the Bible,
Greek and Latin Prefixes and Word Parts,

200 Encouraging Notes from the Bible and
Notes by Philip G. Roets
Biblical Quotations for Each Day of the Year.

Not published at time of Phil's death; Lois will continue the work:
Commentaries on the complete Old and New
Testament using translations from original
languages of Hebrew (OT) and Greek (NT).
Thematic monographs on Biblical topics.
Collections of his newspaper columns.
Wildlife Articles for Students. - nonfiction.
Short works of Fiction.
Excerpts from his personal journals 1979-2002.

Phil and Lois were jointly writing this book so maybe
Lois can finish it.
Book: Leadership Examples in Old and New
Testament: Case Studies.

Not finished at time of Phil's death. Lois cannot complete
these works as they need Phil's brilliant and
creative mind and incredible knowledge:
⌄ More monographs on Biblical issues and themes.
⌄ Fiction based on Phil's wildlife writings.
⌄ Book: Men and Women of the Bible: Why Were
their Stories Included in the Bible?.

*10/29/02. Philip died at 5:45 p.m. at Iowa Methodist Hospital,
Des Moines, Iowa, where he had been since Sept. 25th. -
surgery for bladder cancer. He was recovering when the
surgeon broke a drainage tube while removing it. This
necessitates another surgery, the 3rd in 21 days, to remove
the tube portion that remained in his body. Numerous
complications followed (infections, kidney stone) and
the body could take no more abuse. He died peacefully
with Lois holding his hand.*

At the time of Phil's death,
Phil's favorite gospel was the Gospel According to John.
He was editing/reviewing his commentary on John
the day he was taken to the hospital on a 911 call.

Phil's comfort in his last days was the Good Shepherd. Phil
believed the message of Jesus is the Good Shepherd -
nothing showy nor grand but daily service to others.

Phil's favorites:

Recreation: reading (Grisham, L'Amour); word
puzzles; conversation with family, neighbors,
friends at the post office; TV: Jeopardy, Wheel
of Fortune, Mystery; Movies (videos viewed
at home): Driving Miss Daily, Cool Runnings,
Mighty Ducks, Les Miserables-the 10th
anniversary performance in Albert Hall.

Phil had natural and cultivated appreciation of fine arts.

Music: Two operas he really enjoyed: "Lucia di
Lammermoor" by Donizetti and "The Abduction from
the Seraglio" by Mozart. He also liked Gilbert and
Sullivan's operattas and folk songs like "You Are My
Sunshine." . Phil had a beautiful tenor voice and sang
with joy at Song Fests and Christmas carols at home.

Theater: He appreciated dialogue and ability of performers
to bring life to lines that tell a story. He got a smile
on his face when he remembered the performance
at the outdoor theater in Spring Green, WI, of
Moliere's "Le Tartuffe" and dubbed the lead character
"the pious fraud". He also happily recollected the
performances produced during seminary days.

Artistic expression was always appreciated, especially
sculpture. Rome was filled with sculpture. "The Pieta"
served as a visual guide to understanding Mary's
role as described in the gospels. Phil willingly visited
art museums and appreciated original art. He and
Lois bought art for their home- professionals and
amateurs; studied and completed ceramic works;
admired works created in glass (fragile yet strong)
and photography to record people, events and sights.

*Phil lived a full life of service. He is missed by many. His
good influence lives in many many people around the world.*

Books donated to local libraries "Donated in Memory of Philip G. Roets" (many books in many libraries - thanks!)

Award: Philip G. & Lois F. Roets Award for Developing Leadership Skills in Students, K-12.

Open to: Adults who work with K-12 students/children.
Purpose: To adults to develop leadership skills in students.
Administered by U. Iowa Foundation through the
Belin-Blank International Center for Gifted Education.
Lois is Resource Specialist at this Center for Gifted.
Funded for three years assured, with option beyond 2005.
Want information? Write: Leadership Award.
PO Box 8358   Des Moines, Iowa 50301-8358

Memorial Benches/Plaques to Honor Phil

• Wichita, Kansas. "Leaf" plaque at Botanica. Phil's name will "live" in Wichita - Phil's place of birth.

> In memory of beloved husband,
> **Philip G. Roets** 1921 - 2002.
> from his wife, Lois

• Wichita, Kansas. Memorial Bench in Butterfly Garden of Botanica, Wichita, Kansas.   Inscription:

> **Philip G. Roets,** 1921-2002.
> Author, brother, educator, father, friend, husband,
> linguist, neighbor, priest, Biblical Scholar.
> From his loving wife, Lois F. Roets

• Iowa City, Iowa. Bench on bike/walking trail beside the Iowa River. At this location, you can see "up & down" river. It is beside towering maples. Bald eagles roost here in the winter. Inscription is the same as in Wichita.

• Madison, Wis. Bench: Thai Garden in Olbrich Gardens, Both names are listed as Madison is the favorite city of Phil and Lois. Needs of family occasioned moving to Iowa - native state of Lois. Inscription on bench in Madison:

> **In Honor of**
> **Philip G. and Lois F. Roets**

Memorials to be Established - hope in 2004.

1. Oconomowoc, Wis. Location of major seminary where Philip was educated, ordained, taught seminarians, conducted retreats. The seminary no longer exists. Now the land along Lake LaBelle, on seminary's shoreline, is private property.

2. Pardeeville, Wis. Community north of Madison that gave both of us our first jobs when we left religious life. This memorial will honor both Philip and Lois Roets. Our ties remain to that community as educators, friends and neighbors - since 1969.

3. Philip G. Roets Center for Biblical Studies.
    a. Website: Phil's writings and audio clips from lectures.
    b. Respository of his reference books as a Center
        for scholars and students to use his books.

4. Publications of Phil's unpublished writings - 2004:
A. <u>Death and Fulness of Life.</u>
B. <u>Commentaries on Old and New Testament:</u> book & CD.
    Extensive distribution is planned for convents, seminaries, churches, libraries, members of Catholic Biblical Associatior (Phil was a continuous member since 1952), reading rooms.
C. <u>Monographs (Collection) on Biblical Topics and Themes.</u>
D. <u>"Word to the Wise": Selections from Newspaper Columns</u>
    Phil wrote twice-weekly for Oskaloosa Herald. 1982-1994.
E. <u>Excerpts from Phil's personal journals, 1979-2002,</u>
    on nature, love, Biblical insights, education, wisdom.
F. Collection of greetings/inspiration cards
    Vignettes of wisdom from Phil's journals.

⬇*Items G & H may/may not be "publishable".*
  G. Copies of his Biblical lectures-audio format.
  H. Phil's non-fiction and fiction stories for students.

✍ For information when publications and website are available, contact Lois Roets at:

✉ PO Box 8358 Des Moines, Iowa 50301-8358.

☎ tel: 515-278-4765. fax: 515-270-8303
    email: lroets@uswest.net

We write the

Symphony

of

our lives

which does

not die

any more than the

symphonies of

Beethoven.

Author's Journal. October 26, 1982.

Father Philip G. Roets
- as priest and teacher.

Father Roets and his sister, Cecilia.

Reverend Philip G. Roets CSsR.

Informal picture of Phil with his father and mother:
Philip G. Roets   and   Pauline (Lohkamp) Roets

Mr. Philip G. Roets - as married man and teacher.

Philip G. Roets and
Lois F. (Schelle) Roets

Married: June 7, 1969.

25th Wedding Anniversary.
June, 1994.

School pictures. Pardeeville, Wisconsin. c. 1976.

A Guide to Fulness of Life - Ten Commandments Rewritten.

A STRONG HUMAN SOCIETY! TEN STEP PROGRAM TO LIFE!

Rewritten by Philip G. Roets STL SSL

The Ten Commandments of Moses were concerned primarily with what we were **not** to do! The one commandment of the second Moses, Jesus, tells us what we **are** to do. It is "Love"!

1. God is the goal and the center of life.

2. Respect and honor the family name.

3. Time is a sacred and precious gift. Use it well.

4. Honor your father and your mother; the home is the foundation of society.

5. All of life is sacred and must be respected.

6. Love is the foundation of growth.

7. Property rights are essential to the individual and society.

8. A good reputation is the foundation of a person's self-worth and dignity.

9. Lustful desires are a violation of the other person's dignity.

10. Envy and jealousy over another person's property is self-destructive.